The Ulti.

COSMIC ORDERING

Empower Your Destiny: Take Control of Your Life

Andronicos Andronicou

Cover Art by Sabidesign.co.uk

You may contact the author at
info@cosmicorderingonline.com

ISBN: 978-1-4116-9299-2

www.CosmicOrderingOnline.com

Every universe needs a sun to give it life, Michelle, you are the sun in mine.

Contents

Your Better Life Starts Here!

People are always too busy doing things to take stock of their own life. Either they are too busy studying for a qualification, too busy working to pay the bills, too busy trying to find love, too busy raising children, too busy caring for an elderly parent, or simply too busy being too busy. To a casual observer it may seem that 'busy' people are active with a purpose, the sad truth is that they are like passengers in a rowing boat without a paddle lost at sea. They are just drifting along the river of life, reacting to one circumstance after another. They have absolutely no control over which direction they go, by what means, and what they will see. Being busy helps them hide their lack of purpose from themselves. But, in those rare quiet moments that everyone has a deep problem begins to surface. It first manifest itself as a gnawing on the consciousness of the soul. Then it can almost be heard like a faint tap, tap, tapping sound emanating from within one's body which cannot be identified. Then overpowering feelings without words. Like impatience and yearnings. For the majority of people this emotion is never vocalised. For the rest of their lives, even when they smile, their soul is always burdened with this unspoken sorrow. They spend their life in a permanent state of disaffection.

For the blessed few. This unspoken emotion, gets louder and louder. Like a prisoner trapped inside your heart demanding to be released, banging harder and harder until… One day YOU suddenly wake up, sit up sharply, your mouth opens and you say to yourself *'I want more from life.'*

By picking up *The Ultimate Guide to Cosmic Ordering* you have made a brave and courageous acknowledgment that there are areas of your life that you want to change or improve. Desiring change is not enough, you need knowledge and direction. This book will reveal to you the ancient secrets of Cosmic Ordering. A power so great that you just have to ask the Cosmos for what you really want, and you *will* get it.

There are clear instructions and clear explanations. You will learn how to channel your energy into the Cosmos. You will understand that the wonders of the universe are not to be feared and that your future is *not* set in stone. By using Cosmic Ordering you can take your life in any direction you choose, realise any dream. Improve your personal and professional relationships, change career, increase your wealth, find true love, and absolute fulfilment. Everything that you ever hoped for yourself really can be achieved! For when your head and heart are facing the right direction, and your emotions are fully charged, you will then be able to connect to the Cosmos, achieve your greatest potential and empower your ultimate destiny. Make no mistake about it. This book absolutely is your handbook to a better, healthier, richer, happier, more successful life. Entrust your faith in the greater workings of the Cosmos and you will be *unstoppable*.

The Ultimate Guide to Cosmic Ordering contains powerful subliminal guidance. The most pertinent messages are subtly repeated. The more familiar you become with the text, the greater your spiritual comprehension of the guidance within. This will enable you to connect to the Cosmos better and faster, and to communicate your desires easier, with a greater deal of success.

Music of the Spheres

"As Above, So Below"

- Hermes Trismegistus

Many thousands of years ago when man was more primitive then he is now the world was a different place. Every day was fraught with danger. Wild animals to hunt that preferred to kill and eat rather than be killed and be eaten. Disease that could annihilate a tribe in days, and harsh weather that posed as much danger as wild beasts.

Society was not as it is now. Humans lived in small tribal communities. Before the written word the only way for knowledge to be shared was not by books or computers. People communicated by ancient languages and by descriptive physical gestures. They talked and sang. In fact if they had any knowledge which they felt was vital to pass on to their descendents, the only way to preserve it was via the oral tradition. It was shared directly from one person to another.

There was no one to teach them, no one to guide. Like children stranded on a desert island world without any line of communication. There wasn't any books of faith that provided knowledge or answers, there wasn't any philosophical discussions on whether God is vengeful or loving. There wasn't any guidance, there was nothing. The only explanation they had was when they gazed at the sky by day, and the Sun illuminated the ground, and at night when they gazed and saw the Moon and the stars. Through a primeval instinct they somehow knew, truly *knew*, that somehow in someway, all the questions they had, about the world, the sky, the sea, themselves; all the answers were right there in the stars.

Space is generally regarded by most scientists as being infinite in size. If they don't all agree on it being infinite, they do all agree that it is very, *very* big. It is filled with many different star systems. Our little corner of space is called *the Solar System*, derived from Sol, the Sun's Latin name. The Sun gives life to our system. It is orbited by nine planets including our own. In order they are Mercury, Venus, Earth, Mars, Jupiter, Saturn, Uranus, Neptune, and Pluto.

By stargazing mankind learnt many practical things about Earth & nature, that we take for granted today. It takes 24 hours for the Earth to rotate on its axis once.

It takes 27 ½ days for the Moon to orbit the Earth, and it takes 365 days for the Earth to orbit the Sun. Earth's axis is on a tilt, this means it leans like the *Leaning Tower of Pisa*. Sometimes a country is nearer the Sun, sometimes further away. This gives us the four seasons, their quarterly change, and how this affects the growth of crops. The practical benefits means knowing when to plant crops and when to harvest. It was from this success that mankind then looked to the stars for illumination on their own lives. It was from mankind's need to know more that astrology was born.

Astrology is the study of the movements and positions of the celestial bodies, that is the Sun, the Moon and the planets, to determine a correlation with events on Earth and for the purpose of revealing knowledge and insights on humans' character and affairs. Astonishingly, astrology developed independently in different civilisations. Around 3000BC the Babylonians believed that Earth was created by a god, and that the surrounding universe was created as an accompaniment to it for the purpose of communicating to mankind. Between 3000-2000BC the Babylonians developed a system of celestial portents to interpret the meaning of their god. Around 2000BC China had also developed its own system of astrology; Verdic astrology developed in India, and the Maya of central America also developed their own astrology. Babylonian astrology was to later be incorporated into the teachings in other countries including the Hellenistic astrology of Greece which was later exported to all of Europe, and so the influence of astrology reached all corners of the world.

How does Astrology work? There are many different schools of astrology but they do have certain tenants of teaching which are universal. Standing on Earth looking up. The ecliptic is the perceived plane around the Earth on which the Sun, and the other celestial bodies visible with the naked eye rotate around the Earth. This also includes the Moon, and the planets Mercury, Venus, Mars, Jupiter and Saturn.

The nearby belt of space either side of the ecliptic is called the zodiac. The zodiac is divided into twelve 30 degree segment. These are Aries the Ram, Taurus the Bull, Gemini the Twins, Cancer the Crab, Leo the Lion, Virgo the Virgin, Libra the Balance, Scorpio the Scorpion, Sagittarius the Archer, Capricorn the Goat, Aquarius the Water and Pisces the Fishes. The Sun, the Moon, and the visible planets all pass through the signs of the zodiac. Each star-sign represents a set of human characteristics. For example Cancer represents sensitivity, whilst Leo is representative of a proud and magnanimous character. Whilst the planets are not only named after the gods and goddesses from Greek and Roman mythology, they are said to embody their personality traits. For example Mars exemplifies wars, whilst Venus is the symbol of love and femininity. So when we talk about a person's star sign, this refers to the zodiac sign that the Sun occupied at the moment of their birth.

A horoscope is a chart that maps the position and movements of the celestial bodies the Sun the Moon and the planets and their position in the zodiac at specific times for the purpose of giving insights and meanings to specific peoples' lives and events and thus their *potential* destiny.

In this modern era there has been much debate as to whether the stars and planets really have an effect on what happens down here on Earth. From a purely scientific perspective physicists have been sure of the interaction and co-relationship between Earth and the planets for a long time. Most obviously the Sun is known to bring heat, light and life. Then there is the phenomenon of *Tide Generating Force*. This is when the Moon which is in constant orbit of Earth, exerts a strong gravitational pull on it. This leads to the direct effect of creating tidal action by affecting the currents of Earth's oceans. Additionally there is planetshine as discovered by Leonardo da Vinci in the 1500s. This is when the Sun's light is reflected of one planet on to another, as does happen when it reflects of the Earth on to the Moon.

Just as sure as the Moon affects the currents of the sea, the Moon stars, and certainly the Sun affects the behaviours of all living creatures. In folklore werewolves change form when they see the full Moon. More interestingly is the real phenomena know as the *Lunar Effect*. This is the manner in which the Moon is said to affect the behaviour of people! And other living things. The coral on Australia's Great Barrier Reef spawns four or five days after the full Moon. Moon Mating is when there is a greater desire to have sexual relations during a full Moon. Many farmers and zookeepers attest to this affecting their livestock and other outdoor species. Before the days of artificial light humans were greatly affected by this too. Although there is anecdotal evidence from many a nightclub doormen who will attest this phenomena still exist. One UK survey for a major insurance firm found that there was a fifty percent increase in car accidents during full Moons. And a 2002 study of over 122,000 police reports in Toledo in Ohio USA, found that on the 38 nights there was a full Moon, there was also a 5.5% increase in violent crime.

The correlation between the interaction of the celestial bodies has led renown scientists to search for an explanation. Albert Einstein was a theoretical physicist, and is commonly regarded as the greatest physicist to have ever lived. Renown for his Theory of Relativity and exceptional insights into the laws of Earth, space and the universe. In his later life he worked on the most ambitious theory possible –the *Unified Field Theory*, also known as the *Theory of Everything*. Unified Field Theory is the holy grail of scientific study. So ambitious and audacious is this theory that when discovered, it will *link* the interactions of *all* physical phenomena and matter, (including the effects of the planets on man & vice-versa) *explain* their behaviour and ultimately include an explanation of the origin of the universe! Unfortunately Einstein died before discovering such a theory. Stephen Hawking the world's most famous living theoretical physicist is also searching for a Theory of Everything, and hopes to discover such a theory within the next twenty years. Whilst the theory hasn't been 'discovered' yet it does demonstrate how scientific minds acknowledge that the stars, the planets, Earth, and mankind are all part of an interconnected whole.

So it is the case that mankind looks to the heavens studying its mechanisms. But it is important to note that astrology isn't about understanding the mechanics of the stars, it's really a search for guidance, understanding and answers relating specifically to us as people, women, men and children, and the things that affect us living here on Earth. Thus a pertinent question is are they merely reflective of our characters and events, or is our destiny inevitably entwined with them?… The celestial bodies of the greater Cosmos *do* affect us, and our moods, as well as our interactions with others and the general current of our days. *But!* In an age where even the high-brow non-tabloid papers include peoples' star signs, people take the saying 'written in the stars' too literally. Read your star sign, enjoy it. There is great value in reading what the stars say about you. Your horoscope can give you a clear understanding of the person that you are, your personality, your strengths and your weaknesses. But don't be a slave to your horoscope and auspicious readings, because then you become an instrument of the universe as you become lost in your own body. There is not a book with everyone's name in it, and their birth date, and day of death. We are a product of our environment and Sun signs can and do affect us, but contrary to certain beliefs our destinies are not fixed. *YOUR* destiny is not fixed. Its not set in stone.

The Greek philosopher Socrates said;

"Must we not acknowledge, that in each of us there are the same principles and habits which there are in the state; and that from the individual they pass into the state? — how else can they come there?"

This is an astoundingly powerful statement. It means that just as the greater Cosmos affects man and is reflected in mankind, It also means that;

The Cosmos is reflective of mankind, and mankind can affect and control the Cosmos!

You are not just a vessel of the universe, you are part of it, and *the universe is a vessel of you.* You can call out to it. The planets and environment can affect you and your life. But *this is a two-way process*! We can call out back and 'speak' to them and affect them. This is a great power that every single person has within them, few are aware of it, fewer still are those that try to utilise it. But what you hold in your hands is the first step to improving yourself and your life! You are one of the lucky ones.

Through the power of Cosmic Ordering you now have the means to take control of your life.

Synchronicity – Whispers From Above

Texas USA 1930. On a warm July evening policeman Allan Folby was involved in a car crash. He had damaged the femoral artery in his leg and was facing the very real risk of bleeding to death. A passer-by, Dr Alfred Smith stopped at the accident scene. He took a bandage from his car, wrapped it tightly around Foley's leg and stopped the bleeding. Foley's life was saved and he went on to make a full recovery. Five years later whilst working Folby arrived at a crash scene. He found a man bleeding to death from a damaged femoral artery. He saved the man's life. The man was Dr Alfred Smith.

Everyday enthusiastic scientists continue to make 'discoveries' about how our universe works and the scientific laws by which it operates. They share with us 'new' knowledge on why the rain falls, or how the sun shines, or why winds blow. Or they make inventions to reflect light, or open tins with one hand, or thin coats that warm you in the cold. So its no wonder that they tend to view themselves as the ultimate examples of wise men and women who are there to guide the masses. Yet the average person living in the 21st century tends to have a more lackadaisical approach. When we hear about a new discovery, yes its interesting, yes its insightful but ultimately it doesn't have any bearing on the mundane state of our ordinary lives. We just plod on. Doing what we're doing.

Likewise when its comes to matters of faith. In our cynical times, having a deep belief in God is admirable. Yet there are those zealots who feel it is their purpose to masticate over the smallest details of their religion. They profess to know anything and everything from why 'hope is a sin,' the exact patriarchal order in the kingdom of heaven, to telling us which saints and angels are closest to the ear of God, as well as describing the decorations and colour scheme of heaven! This is crazy! Yes we have faith that we are part of a greater whole, but sometimes, and its very understandable why...

We only believe what we see

That's why many people have difficulty believing in a supreme being. How many times have you heard someone say something like;

"Do I believe in God? Let me put it this way, when I meet him I will shake his hand, until then I think I've got more chance of meeting the Easter bunny dressed in a ra-ra skirt."

Likewise many believers pray, regularly attending their place of worship. But sometimes, normally during one's darkest hour, (and you may have experienced this) a person might be praying hard to God. Something in their life is causing them pain and sadness, tears in their eyes, sobbing, head on the ground and in their darkest hour they take their last vestige of dignity and pray for *his* voice to calm, pray for *his* hand to guide, pray for themselves then... they stop. Slowly look up. Look around at each of the four walls. Then up to the ceiling. They are then overcome with the most horrifying feeling to beset a believer. The feeling that God isn't listening. Because he isn't there. Because he doesn't exist.

The problem arises from the fact that we live in the age of science & computers. For every physical event that happens there has to be a scientific law to explain it.

Again it comes down to the fact that we are taught to only believe what we see. Perhaps, we are being too reckless. In an age of science and computers and rules, and laws, and proof, where scientists like to neatly match questions with universally accepted answers - occasionally a spanner gets in the works. Strange little coincidences that seem to be more than just random events. There seems to be *intent* and *meaning* behind them.

On the 5th December 1664 a ship sunk on the shores of Wales. On the 5th of December 1785 another ship went down on the same location. And on the 5th December 1866 a third ship went down at exactly the same spot. Each ship had only one survivor. In each case the survivor's name was Hugh Williams.

Have you ever been thinking of an old friend or relative who you have had no contact with for some time and completely out of the blue they telephone you, or you bump into them in the street? Have you ever experienced a time in your life when you have experienced financial hardships, with difficulty paying for food and other living costs? Then completely unforeseen a person who owes you money pays you back? Have you ever been faced with a decision that you have to make, unsure of what you have to do, you then hear something an unrelated stranger says that helps you decide? If you have, then you have experienced *synchronicity*.

In 1949, Swiss psychologist Carl Jung created the term synchronicity to describe what he called *'coincident occurrences of acausal events.'* In other words, an event that apparently happens by happenstance but on closer examination by the parties concerned appears to have some significance to it, regardless of whether they can interpret its meaning or not. Carl Jung developed his theories on synchronicity at the age of 68 after he slipped on some ice, broke his ankle and suffered a heart attack. Whilst recovering from a life threatening fever he began to perceive the world differently. As is the case with those who undergo a near-death experience and survive. Or those who use narcotic stimulants for 'recreational purposes.' Jung experienced an altered state of consciousness. He saw little twists of fate which seemed to reveal a loose seam of the universe that has been left hanging. He saw evidence of *patterning* in the world. Little coincidences which seemed to be more than just chance because it appeared that there was a *meaning* behind them. This in itself is an amazing revelation because synchronicity means that *something* is going on.

In 359 BC the Greek physician Hippocrates said;

"There is a link, there is a bond, so to speak, and even so-called inanimate objects have a form of communication. In other words the whole universe is a living breathing entity and its various life forms, in all the kingdoms, animal, plant, mineral, human, are not as removed from each other as previously thought."

Which can be a difficult concept to grasp until you realise that it means that in the Cosmos all people, all physical matter, all energy, is interconnected.

In his book 'Les Huguenots' the French poet Emile Deschamps recalled how in 1805 as a child he once shared a table with the stranger Monsieur de Fontgibu. During his travels to England Fontgibu had developed a taste for plum pudding. He bought some and implored Emile Deschamps to sample it. Ten years passed, and an adult Deschamps came across a restaurant near the Paris opera that made plum pudding. He'd only ever eaten it that one time but remembering how he found it delicious he ordered a piece only to be told the last slice had been reserved for another customer. A waiter then informed him the other guest had kindly offered to share the last piece with him. He went over to the customer only to see it was Fontgibu. Both men were absolutely flabbergasted to find that plum pudding had led to their meeting again. Several years later in 1832 Deschamps was a guest at a dinner party. He was delighted to learn that the desert was plum pudding. He then regaled his friends with the astonishing tale of his two encounters with Fontgibu and the plum pudding, and joked that only Fontgibu was missing from his plum pudding dining experience. Moments later having entered the wrong floor of the building Monsieur de Fontgibu stepped in the room. Deschamps said "On three occasions I have eaten plum pudding, and on each occasion I have seen Monsieur Fontgibu. My hair stood up on my head!"

The plum pudding story illustrates synchronicity at its most obscure. A sequence of events so far beyond chance and probability yet having no apparent meaning or purpose. Alternatively synchronicity manifests itself via portents, signs or omens, to offer a person guidance or direction when they are most in need. Most often when a person has to make an important decision in life.

Synchronicity sometimes takes a more explicit role in peoples' lives when it lends a helping hand. As in the case of the car accident with Dr Alfred Smith saving the life of Allan Folby only to have Folby return the favour. But - and this is profound. If synchronicity is providing guidance, and direction and help, it then stands to reason that there is a guiding _intelligent force_ behind it! An intelligent force that is omnipresent and all knowing. In our everyday lives even the most religious don't have two-way conversations with God in the literal sense. Yet if you look out for evidence of it, you may be able to read its messages and use them for guidance in your own life. Heed the signs, use the flow, tune into the Cosmos, because in this realm, synchronicity is the nearest that you will get to communicating with a _higher power_.

What is Your Destiny? -And do you Want It?

"Every man has his own destiny: the only imperative is to follow it, to accept it, no matter where it leads him."

- Henry Miller

By investing in the knowledge held within this book you have already demonstrated that there are things in your life that you want, that you do not have, things that you desire. Why? Why do you desire more? Why do you want these things? Why should you make changes? Why do you think you should change?

Ask yourself *'What is my life like. Am I happy with it?'* If words can sum up how you feel about your entire life, your answer may vary from 'life is bad' to 'life is great.' Although most likely you feel that your life falls somewhere between the two. Well, if you were asked *'how would you feel if your current situation in life, personal, work, financial and social was to remain as it is until the day you die would you be happy about it?'* If you knew you couldn't change a thing you would probably be horrified. Not because your life is so very bad, but because within you is an innate feeling and hope that in your life you will do more and achieve more. Even if you are the most cynical of people there are times, however fleeting, however rare, that you truly believe that you have the fantastic potential to achieve greatness in all areas of your life. Know this;

Every single person on this planet has the potential to achieve greatness – including you.

Everybody! Not just the good, the keen, and the motivated but also the lazy and the immoral. The reason is that every single person has a destiny. Well, what is destiny?

Dictionaries tend to describe destiny as being a fate that is set and unchangeable- but this isn't quite correct.

Your destiny is to strive to realise your dreams, and achieve your ultimate potential.

You hold within you the promise of being the very best version of yourself that you can possibly be.

"Destiny is not a matter of chance, it is a matter of choice; it is not a thing to be waited for, it is a thing to be achieved."

-William Jennings Bryan

What is Cosmic Ordering? & How Does It Work?

Everyone hopes and dreams. But when you actively pursue a dream in the belief that you will actually realise it, it becomes a *Destiny-Goal*. Destiny-Goals are goals in your life that you want to attain. These may be to attain material goods and wealth or Destiny-Goals can be achieving success in other aspects of your life such as improving your physical state or building a happy family.

The Cosmos is *everything*. It is all that exist, from the smallest subatomic particle under a scientist microscope to the most humongous planets on corners of the universe that will never be discovered. The Cosmos encompasses *everything* in existence – and *more*. It is derived from the Greek word *Kos-mos* meaning order or harmony. Although human minds can only dream of its workings, what we can perceive is that everything and everyone is connected in some form of creational arrangement.

Somewhere, out there, within the Cosmos is a *higher power* at work with intelligence and purpose. Imagine if you will, the Cosmos as an infinite swirling mass. It is all around us, above us, below us and *inside* us. It can divide us, but most importantly it can bind us.

It is a mysterious, powerful, and unexplainable force that can be used for good to better our own lives, and those of everyone around us.

Cosmic Ordering is when you spiritually connect to the Cosmos to divulge the innermost secrets of your heart,

Cosmic Ordering is when you ask the Cosmos to use its energy its powers to make your Destiny-Goals a reality.

Trying to understand the concept of the Cosmos is understandably bewildering. But if we look at it in terms that more easily relate to our everyday lives, it can make things a little simpler to comprehend.

Think of the Cosmos as a social club where every single person in the world is automatically an enrolled member. The benefits are that you get unlimited personal support and guidance for any aspect of your life, and you get to ask for any gift you want and you will get it! The only proviso is that you regularly attend the club and willingly participate in all the activities held there. Likewise with Cosmic Ordering you *will* get whatever you ask the Cosmos for, but it is a constant sea-sawing process whereby you and the Cosmos are responding to one another, and where you have certain actions and commitments to partake. First you must communicate with the Cosmos so that you can ask it for what you want. You will learn exactly how to do this in the chapter *The 7 Stages of Cosmic Ordering.*

Your thoughts are your direct channel of communication with the Cosmos. From time to time everyone has their head in the clouds as they wonder what their life might be like under different circumstances. However the Cosmos doesn't respond to flights of fancy that your thoughts might take. The Cosmos responds to firm definite Destiny-Goals. How you think, and what you think about directly affects your ability to connect to the Cosmos. Thus you have to control your thoughts, or at the very least steer them in the direction of your ambitions. Move away from pessimistic thoughts about what you lack, and move nearer beliefs that are optimistic about what you will gain. When you consistently focus your thoughts and feelings on these ambitions you become *Destiny-Goal conscious.* It becomes a motivational force that inspires your emotions. Your mind will want to make your desires a reality. When you want something so much, believe it so much, your heart shouts out to the Cosmos. When this happens the Cosmos listens! It hears you, it understands your desires, it understands you, and it *answers* you!

There are a number of different ways in wish the Cosmos can grant you your Destiny-Goals. The most straightforward but *least common* way is that what you asked for suddenly comes into your life. So if you asked for wealth you suddenly win on the lottery, or win at the races, or a cheque is fortuitously sent to you. Or if you wish to find love the next day you literally bump into someone who will become the love of your life. Cosmic Orders that fall into your lap like this are often quite rare but are the most powerful.

More commonly the Cosmos, after hearing your Destiny-Goals, will try to give you a gentle but pronounced nudge in the right direction via synchronicity. This can be via portentous signs giving you guidance on what to do, what not to do, or what or whom to avoid. Learning to recognise instances of synchronicity will benefit you in this regard. However you mustn't allow yourself to fall victim to sign-searching whereby you are too afraid to make decisions without the aid of signs. In life do not try and see meaning where there is none. With time and wisdom, whenever you are given synchronicitous sign you will be absolutely sure of it - how you interpret it is what matters!

The Cosmos will also aid you in more subtle means when it works *through you* to influence your behaviours and decisions. For instance if you make a Cosmic Order to gain wealth, the Cosmos will make your conscious mind more alert to the value of opportunities that come your way, or more informed when you have to make an important decision.

When you entwine yourself with the Cosmos by opening up your communication channels with others you are more attentive to prospects, more open to new experiences, and more willing to talk to other people and listen to them, the Cosmos will reward you handsomely by giving you firm and clear guidance on what you need to do to make your Destiny-Goals a reality.

The most direct way that the Cosmos grants your Orders is when it subtly changes the world around you in your favour. This might mean that when you are desperately in need of some money you get a 'fluky hand' in a game of Blackjack. Or when you are in a mad rush to drive to the other side of town all the traffic lights happen to be green, or perhaps in a contest you do everything right whilst your competitors happen to do everything wrong. Such direct intervention by the Cosmos goes unnoticed, except for the nagging feeling that a minor miracle has happened. Some may interpreted this as 'being lucky' or even claim to be 'blessed.' However you choose to describe it what is evident is a powerful shift of reality that directly benefits you in your pursuit of your Destiny-Goals.

John Goodspeed has long pursued a career with the company GreatLifeCareer Ltd. without much success, failing to secure an interview or even a rejection letter. He then fully follows the seven-stage instructions for Cosmic Ordering in order to realise his Destiny-Goal of working for GreatLifeCareer Ltd. The Cosmos 'hears' his Order. Circumstances which were unfavourable subtly becoming favourable. The Human Resources Officer who reviews GreatLifeCareer Ltd job applications may have previously been too busy to notice John's résumé had fallen down the back of the filing cupboard... But now she notices it, and is especially drawn to it. John Goodspeed is invited to an interview. Not being very punctual he is late leaving his house meaning he will be too late to catch the bus and so will miss his interview and blow his opportunity. But something peculiar happens. The bus is involved in an unusual series of traffic incidents, thus delaying it slightly. Oblivious to it all, John arrives at the bus stop just as the bus does. When he gets off the bus he walks down a busy road towards the office. He overhears a newspaper vendor give a woman directions 'Just stick to the right side of the road.' Although this bit of information is totally unrelated to his journey he sees that just ahead the pavement gets narrower and there is a very large, long, and probably quite deep, puddle next to it. So John crosses the road and looks back to where he was walking. A van then drives through the puddle. If John had not crossed the road he would now be covered in muddy water. Whew! He gets to the GreatLifeCareer Ltd offices on time, breezes through the interview, and is rewarded with his dream job.

What do you Want?
-NO! What do you *Really* Want?

When you have Destiny-Goals you use the power of Cosmic Ordering to realise them. But before you allow yourself to *connect* to the Cosmos. *Stop.* Because when you make Cosmic Orders for their power to be effective, they must be true to you, your personality, and come from your heart. It's imperative that you are clear that what you *think* you want is not necessarily the same as what you *actually* want. This isn't as condescending as it sounds! If you ask ten people if they could have whatever they want, what would they wish for? Nine out of the ten would probably say millions in their bank account (and the other person would probably say billions). Is this really this case? Are people really that shallow? That all they desire is wealth and money? *Yes?!* Don't rush to say 'yes!' Although people may have the same desires, such as attaining wealth, their motivations for these desires often vary greatly.

By examining the motivations behind your desires you will find out what you truly want.

For instance if you want great wealth because you are fed up of renting and want a home of your own. This means that your Destiny-Goal is to own your own property. If you want great wealth so that you have the freedom to pay for an around-the-world trip to see famous landmarks and people. This means your Destiny-Goal is to travel. Or perhaps you have wondered how having the *fame* of a celebrity would bring you public adoration. Perhaps you feel underappreciated or unloved. Thus your Destiny-Goal could be to achieve more in your professional life, and form new relationships, and/or find love in your personal life.

Whilst the media constantly portray Hollywood images of happiness as having fame and money. Yet there seems to be a contradiction in that many of these celebrities with lives that are promoted as perfect, in fact have a number of problems. Substance abuse, alcohol addiction, drug addiction, sex addiction, and normally a series of broken relationships, as well as regularly requiring psychotherapy. People are naturally humble creatures, and the incentive behind most of our actions is the pursuit of happiness. Whether it be something as pure as a parent watch their child learn something new, or more ambitious such as a entrepreneur seeking world-wide success for their business.

So when thinking about your Destiny-Goals think about what makes you happy. You have got to take the time to examine what *you* really want. Don't decide now. Stop and think about it. Like a mathematician with a problem. Mull it over. Think about it for a week. Consider your professional life, your personal life, your wealth, and the people and the world around you.

Be true to yourself. Don't suppress your inner desires that are an intrinsic part of you (unless they are criminal, violent or criminally violent.) Don't deny what's true about you to make others happy. What makes you laugh? What's your greatest ambition? *What makes you happy?* Let your thoughts hopes and dreams soar for a week.

Your heart contains your innermost hopes and aspirations. Perhaps you have kept them secret because you feel that they are nothing more than vanity. Perhaps you don't respect these inner goals because you 'live in the real world.' What this actually means is that in your mind, you cannot realistically perceive how you can realise these dreams! You have lacked the confidence, but don't let this stop you! If you honestly knew that you could achieve anything you wanted to in your life, what would you like to do? You can do anything that you have a *burning passion* to do, to achieve. Within reason, *anything is possible.* The best clichés are the truest. But know this! The first day of the rest of your life begins right here, right now! Then when you know what your own personal Destiny-Goals are, no matter how unlikely they seem or how difficult to attain, you have made progress! When you have your own personal Destiny-Goals in your sights, fix your gaze on them, reach out to them and clutch them tightly. Because when you know what you want. You are ready to use the awesome power of Cosmic Ordering!

The 7 Stages of Cosmic Ordering

"A certain power to alter things indwells in the human soul and subordinates the other things to her, particularly when she is swept into a great excess of love of hate or the like. When therefore the human soul falls into a great excess of any passion, it can be proved by experiment that the excess binds things together magically and alters them in the way it wants. Whoever would learn the secret of doing and undoing these things must know that everyone can influence everything magically if he falls into a great excess." – Saint Albert the Great

Cosmic Ordering is the process where you communicate with the Cosmos to make your Destiny-Goals a reality. Through the infinite energy of Cosmic Ordering you are going to be able to change anything and everything possible in your life. You will declare to the Cosmos exactly what you want, and you can be sure, that in one form or another, you will get it. Be under no illusions. Cosmic Ordering is a not a complicated process. What is a challenge is that you remain Destiny-Goal focused. You have to be certain that you have the desire, tenacity, and the passionate hunger to pursue your Destiny-Goals…

Stage 1 – Write a Detailed Plan in your personal Cosmic Ordering Journal

You will need to make a full and thorough detailed written plan for you Destiny-Goals. To do this you will first need to find yourself a Cosmic Ordering Journal. A Cosmic Ordering journal is a book used solely for the purpose of transcribing a full and detailed plan of all your Destiny-Goals. The physical form of the journal is entirely down to your discretion. Choose whatever book you feel is right for you, no matter how unusual or quirky. At its most basic level this can be a few sheets of paper stapled together, or a small book traditionally used by school children for writing essays. Or a diary passed its use-by date but full of space, or it could even be a large oversized scrapbook. You may even choose a thick tome, heavy in weight, with luxurious quality paper so that you may write elegantly with a quill. Choose anything you want, but do choose carefully for the journal will hold your inner most secrets - your Destiny-Goals. Hold it close to your bosom, stroke it, kiss it, love it, spray perfume on it. This is the key to the door that will lead you out to your freedom to your future progress, your success and your destiny. Treasure it.

WARNING. Don't allow yourself to get caught up in your journal's monetary value. The cheaper the better. Journals encrusted with gold and diamonds are best avoided. Its value to you should not be in its value as a physical object. Its value is that it holds your Destiny-Goals. So even if the journal is lost or destroyed you shouldn't let it phase you one iota. Because when you know your own Destiny-Goals, they burn so strongly in your heart and soul that it should be easy to transcribe them again.

Imagine you have lived a very long life and had a lot of birthdays. A real lot. You feel you have less than a year on this Earth so you decide to throw the ultimate birthday party in honour of yourself! You're not too bothered by the details but what you do know is that you want lots of people you care about to be there; as well as the desire to have laughter, happiness, a lot of presents, and your loved ones to share and enjoy the food and music with you.

So you arrange the party, and send out the invites to everyone you love and care about. Best friends, close family, your special someone. The day comes. You are at home and keenly wait for your guests. You wait. You wait some more. You wait further still. Your excitement and anticipation soon evaporates. Standing by yourself. With no one there. No music. No food. No cards. No presents. No guests. You become consumed by melancholy. Midnight approaches. Standing cold and alone in the garden you wonder what has happened as you had such high hopes for the day. You then realise that you forgot to call the caterer, you never booked a band, you made a mess of the marquee, and worst of all, you didn't put stamps on the invites. With a heart heavy with sadness you sit down in your chair. Tears stream from your eyes. In little more than a murmur you breathlessly utter 'It wasn't supposed to be like this.' You then close your eyes for the very last time.

Once you have your Cosmic Ordering journal its important to then write a detailed plan for each of your Destiny-Goals. You may think that knowing what you want is enough, but without a clear focus and direction a Destiny-Goal becomes as idol as a daydream. Your brain is fed with so many bits of information during a day, that your detailed plan is a means to alert your subconscious to the significance of the words within. The very act of writing down your Destiny-Goals kick-starts your subconscious' communication with the outside world and the Cosmos.

Firstly, you should begin your Cosmic Order with a *commanding* statement such as *'I ask of the Cosmos…'* or *'I Order from the Cosmos…'* Then write what you want in full detail., not just the name but a full description. So if you want a Jaguar car instead of writing down 'I Order from the Cosmos a new Jaguar car.' Instead write down 'I Order from the Cosmos a new Jaguar sports car. Model XK8. With a metallic Blue colour paint. Cool cream interior. CD and MP3 player on the dashboard. Easy grip steering wheel.' Or if you want a particular career don't just state the job title. State the details of the actual career. The day to day duties of the position. The company that you want to work for. The salary, the perks, the promotional prospects. Or if you want a new home don't just write 'I Order from the Cosmos a new home' instead write 'I Order from the Cosmos a new apartment in the city by the riverside docks with a great view of the sun and the sea. I want the apartment to be a penthouse, with three bedrooms each with fur-style carpets, marble floors in the modern kitchen, high ceilings with crystal chandeliers, and in the living room a giant mural of Marcel Marceau performing a mime of a quixotic crowd.'

More than that you have to write down a timeframe for when you want your Cosmic Order. So you may add that you want your Order in the short term, which is anything from a day to a year, the medium term which is anything over a year to five years, or the long term, which is anytime over five years . You can then compliment your Cosmic Ordering journal with pictures that can inspire your pursuit of your Destiny-Goals. For instance you may be reading a Sunday newspaper supplement and you see a picture of a boat you want, cut it out and paste it in your journal – its in these instances that a big journal can be very useful. Or if you have hopes of finding love and marrying, you may see a picture of a couple on their wedding day. Cut out the picture, put it in your book. Maybe you can add an old picture of yourself, cut out the face, and stick it on the bride or groom to really see the marriage happening for you. Okay, you may well be behaving a bit like a stalker, but so what you're dealing with destiny!

<u>Order what you want, not what you want to leave behind.</u>

Make sure you that you don't make a Cosmic Order using negative language. So if you are struggling financially don't say 'I Order from the Cosmos that *I don't want* to be poor' because the brain tends to ignore the small but important joining word 'don't.' Instead, all its hears is 'I want to be poor.' Likewise avoid writing 'I Order from the Cosmos that I don't want to be alone.' Although it may be a genuine sentiment, with Cosmic Ordering, as with many things in life, you will have more success if you look to the positives. So when ordering say 'I want to be rich...' or 'I want to be share a great social life with many close friends...'

Also when making Cosmic Orders for a change in personal feelings or personal attitudes use the present tense when writing. For instance you may have been through some emotionally difficult times which have left you feeling burdened by sorrow. So you make a Cosmic Order to be happy in the future 'I Order from the Cosmos that I will be happy within a year.' Why wait a year? Make a Cosmic Order to be happy now. '*I Order from the Cosmos that I am happy now.*' This wont change the facts that have led to your sorrows, it does mean that it will enable you to start to immediately develop a more positive and happy mindset. If you think happy you will be happier. This has the immediate effect of making you more in tune to the energies and the power of the Cosmos.

When writing down your Destiny-Goals remember that they are one hundred percent specific to you. They come from you and you are an individual. So try to avoid writing in a style that is sterile, unreservedly factual, and akin to an accountancy report. Your Destiny-Goals come from your emotions so when writing about them infuse your words with these same emotions. 'I Order from the Cosmos that I will have a *wonderful* holiday in the country. It will be so *relaxing* when I walk through the idyllic greenery, eating *delicious* foods at *welcoming* restaurants and meeting *fabulous* people.'

Your detailed plan should *not* be a plan on *how* to achieve your Destiny-Goal. Just write down the details of *what* you want to achieve. So when writing in your Cosmic Ordering journal feel free to write about any Destiny-Goal that you have. Remember, the language that you use is crucial because it enables your brain to understand, and then your heart, so that you have the spiritual and emotional charge to connect to the Cosmos.

Stage 2 – Visualise your Destiny-Goal

After you write down your Destiny-Goals in your Cosmic Ordering journal you have to visualise them. Not just as a vague concept detached from you, but as a clear and absolute reality with you as a part of it. Firstly take the time to close your eyes and envisage your Destiny-Goal with you at the heart of it. If, for example, your Destiny-Goal is to own your own apartment, visualise it with all the detail that you put into your written plan and more. Now see yourself there in the apartment. Walking around. Looking at the décor, admiring it. But try to *visualise* with as many of your five senses as is pertinent. *See*, but also *hear* the sound of your footsteps on the floor. *Feel* the touch of the furniture against your skin. *Smell* the fresh scent of the paint. *Taste* the flavour of a meal in your new kitchen.

Or if your Destiny-Goal is to find a new boyfriend or girlfriend, then *see* yourself standing next to a new partner. *Feel* their hand on your face, *smell* their aftershave or perfume, *hear* the warmth in their voice for you. The process is not too dissimilar to lucid daydreaming, in which you choose to dream what you want. The brain understands pictures and images best. That's why when you watch a poignant film it makes you feel sad, perhaps even cry. Why do people cry even when they know its not real, its just a fictional story played by actors?! Its because on one level the brain perceives the film to be 'real' and so your feelings and emotions respond accordingly to the stimulus. On a subconscious level you don't just *want* your Destiny-Goal to be real, *you need it to be real*, because on a subliminal level you actually *believe its real*. How does this work? After you visualise your Destiny-Goal, and stop to return to the real world. Your brain detects that your Destiny-Goal is missing from reality. So your subconscious tries to address this inconsistency by calling out to the Cosmos. There is a imperceptible communication between your mind, your body, and the Cosmos. A two-way process. Your mind is requesting of the Cosmos to modify reality so that your Cosmic Order is realised. The Cosmos then makes indiscernible and subtle shifts to events and behaviours around you.

Stage 3 - Emotionally charge your Destiny-Goal

Visualising your Destiny-Goal allows you to see yourself in a new changed reality where your Destiny-Goal has been achieved. Visualising with your five senses allows you to *perceive* how things will change. You see how things could be. But the fundamental point is that you need to really *believe* that things will change and are changing. As with the Old Testament bible story of God making man out of clay then breathing on him to bring him to life. You have to charge your visualisations by breathing on to them with the *burning passion* of your emotions. So if your Destiny-Goal is a much larger bank balance then see yourself with a big cheque book in your pocket. See how relaxed you *feel* about paying bills, going on vacation, buying gifts and so on. Spending will be a *pleasure*. Knowing you can afford what you want will make you *feel* more *confident*. When you are financially independent you will *feel proud*.

Stage 4 – Talk to the Cosmos

A Destiny-Goal is just a fanciful idea if you value it one day, and the next you let the wind blow it away from you. If you want your Destiny-Goals to happen, *really* want them to happen, then you have to nurture them so that they grow and become entwined with your character. You have to become *Destiny-Goal conscious* twenty-four hours a day, seven days a week. To the point where it almost becomes an obsession. Your Cosmic Ordering journal, your visualisations, and emotionalising means you have an absolute understanding of your Destiny-Goals. Now you have to directly speak to the Cosmos to 'ask' for all your Destiny-Goals to come true. Although the word 'ask' is used loosely as really its more of a statement of your intentions.

The best time to speak to the Cosmos is early in your morning, and last thing at night. Find a time and place where you will not be disturbed, and try to settle on it as this must be made a daily routine. Get your Cosmic Ordering journal and either read it aloud or simply hold.

Then close your eyes and actually talk to the Cosmos, as if you are having a conversation. You may feel awkward doing this in a room with only yourself but carry on regardless. Whisper if it helps you feel less self-conscious. State your Destiny-Goals. State why you want them and when you want them. Don't just ask for what you want, *declare* what you want. *Demand* it. Loudly, proudly, emphatically!

This process when consistently used focuses the thoughts of your subconscious mind on your Destiny-Goals. The process means you are continually communicating with the Cosmos about what you desire. The Cosmos is working to make Destiny-Goals a reality. You become a conduit for the energies of the Cosmos, and in part, the Cosmos works *through* you to manifest your desires.

So when speaking to the Cosmos in the morning think about what *you* will do during the day to bring you nearer to your Destiny-Goals. This doesn't mean that you have to have a solid concrete action plan but it does mean making very small steps. Perhaps a phone call to enquire about an education course, or buy a magazine dealing with personal finance, or send a card to someone you want to get to know a bit better. Then at the end of the day when you have your final chat with the Cosmos think about what you did, didn't, or could have done to bring you nearer to your Destiny-Goal. Occasionally, when you are so engrossed you can talk, or at least think about it until you fall asleep.

Why do you actually have to *do* anything?

You may well enjoy the comfort of sitting in bed reading the latest book recommended by Oprah Winfrey and munching on doughnuts. But your Destiny-Goal is less likely to materialise. You have to *interact* with the world.

The consistency and length of time which you talk to the Cosmos directly affects its response to you.

Talk regularly and consistently and the Cosmos will always be listening. How successful your Cosmic Orders are relates directly to how regularly you talk.

Stage 5 – Destiny-Symbols

Throughout the day, especially if you are busy it can be all too easy to overlook your thoughts regarding your Destiny-Goals. Whilst it would be somewhat extreme to stipulate that you must fixate solely on this, it is important to give your unconscious mind a gentle reminder. So that even when you are tied up with other things, you are always mindful that you are on a journey that will lead to the fulfilment of your Destiny-Goals. Such reminders are called Destiny-Symbols. A Destiny-Symbol can be any small object of your choice that has a special significance to you as you associate it with achieving your Destiny-Goals.

The least conspicuous and easiest to carry is a necklace or bracelet with a pendant at the end. So if you have a Destiny-Goal to travel to the other side of the world, you might choose a pendent with an aeroplane on it, or perhaps a pendent with St John the patron saint of travellers. Alternatively you can carry with you a compact picture which also serves as a Destiny-Symbol. So if you have your heart set on acquiring a particular yacht carry a small picture of it with you always. Keep it close to you always. Whether this be an inside pocket, or wallet, or handbag.

You can even put it on exposed part of your body so that your Destiny-Symbol can freely see the stars above. Whenever you get an opportunity. Stop, take a good look at your Destiny-Symbol and repeat to yourself your Destiny-Goals. In this way you are always *Destiny-Goal conscious* and always in communication with the Cosmos.

Stage 6 - Send your Order

Sending your Order, is when you directly communicate your Cosmic Order with the outside world. Doing so is an explicit acknowledgement that exterior forces have an effect on your Destiny-Goals and means that when the Cosmos brings you opportunities and circumstances that will bring you closer to your Destiny-Goals you will recognise them, and be receptive to them, and be able to act on them. One of the best ways is to write your Order on a piece of paper. Seal it in a bottle and throw it out to sea. Watch it float out away. Another way is to write your Order on a postcard addressed to *Ultimate Cosmic Ordering, Destiny-Goal Processing Department*. You don't need to write your full name, and you don't need to be too concerned that it hasn't got a full address on it. Be content that it will be read at a postal sorting office by staff that are both confused and bemused.

When you send your Orders out into the world you acknowledge that the Cosmos is listening.

Stage 7 - Have Faith

The seventh stage of Cosmic Ordering takes the least effort but can be the most difficult. All you have to do is have *faith*. Faith in the Cosmos, faith in the people around you, and, most importantly, faith in yourself. Faith and belief is what makes humanity such a powerful force. Because it allows us to look beyond the limitations of our own spheres of knowledge of the world, and by doing so we are able see new spheres, and add new knowledge to what we know. This is progress.

Little over a century ago, if a person proclaimed that humans would be able to one day take to the sky like birds, the concept would have sounded so outlandishly ridiculous, that people would have thought them to be either a drunkard or mentally ill. So inventors of the day didn't even bother to experiment with flying machines as they thought flight would be impossible. But two brothers from the USA, Orville and Wilbur Wright, had a genuine belief that humans travelling in the sky would one day be possible. They didn't know *how* it would be, they just had *faith* that it would be possible. They made it their Destiny-Goal to invent a flying machine. Sometimes they questioned their Destiny-Goal. But their belief meant they experimented with flight where others hadn't. It was this strong *faith* that allowed them to persist and invent a flying machine!

When using the power of Cosmic Ordering its natural to have questions about the whole process. *Does it work? Will it work for me?* And so on. To question is fine and its right. *You* are not omnipresent, accept that you cannot know everything. You cannot always see the full picture. But just because you don't understand exactly how Cosmic Ordering works, whatever happens, don't allow your questions and lack of understanding to stop you from using Cosmic Ordering. Persist! It may be that you have used Cosmic Ordering and are impatient to see results. Or you may have followed the instructions, written down your Destiny-Goals done everything, followed every step of Cosmic Ordering and are curious to know when your Destiny-Goals will be realised. For instance you may be waiting for a particular opportunity that will mean you get to work abroad in an environment that is more stimulating and more financially beneficial. But when it doesn't materialise and you can't see results, you then feel despondent. You then question whether Cosmic Ordering is working for you.

Or you may judge a situation to be bad, circumstances to be wrong, and be unable to comprehend when if ever you will make your Destiny-Goal a reality.

Accept that you cannot see the full picture!
The Cosmos is working in your favour unseen!

What you judge to be a terrible and bad situation may actually be a golden opportunity. 'Your darkest hour' may lead you to meeting a person who becomes a lifelong friend that will bring you strength and companionship when you need it most. But as a mortal you cannot see what the Cosmos will bring you or when. Nor do you have to know how, exactly, the Cosmos works. Focus on your Destiny-Goal, and when you have questions that go unanswered just have a little bit of *faith*.

Miracles

"There are only two ways to live your life. One is as though nothing is a miracle. The other is as though everything is a miracle"

– Albert Einstein

When you harness the power of Cosmic Ordering you are able to take your dreams and make them a reality. But what is the extent of this power? Are there any limitations? Is anything really possible? Can you use Cosmic Ordering to make miracles happen? Well, it all depends on what you classify as a miracle.

Traditionally a miracle is viewed as an unexplainable change in the rules of nature through divine intervention. What this means is that anything that breaks the rules of science and nature is a miracle. When a person loses an arm in an accident this is likely to devastate them and they decide they want it back! They make a Cosmic Order for their arm to grow back! Unfortunately, no matter how well they follow the Seven Stages of Cosmic Ordering it will never grow back.

Likewise you cannot change the rules of human mortality. You may have lost someone very dear to you. You may be living in a miasma of grief, and willing them to return. But you cant wish the dead back to life. (Whilst there may be an army of spiritualist who take exception to this statement they will agree – that if the dead do return, its not in quite the same way as when they were alive...)

The power of Cosmic Ordering cannot alter the laws of nature.

Then there is the more modern interpretation of what is a miracle. These are not miracles in the traditional sense, rather it's an event that is extremely unlikely.

"It would be a miracle if I won a million on the lottery."

" It would be a miracle if I could find the one."

" It would be a miracle if I ever got that promotion."

A woman with one leg completes her Destiny-Goal to run a full 26 mile marathon. A young boy growing up in squalid conditions has a Destiny-Goal to live like a prosperous and important businessman. He propels himself to become an entrepreneur and a Captain of Industry. These are not miracles. These are exemplary achievements. If the woman, or the boy had perceived their Destiny-Goals as impossible, they would not have pursued them. There is a difference between the improbable and the impossible. When you can differentiate between the two it is tremendously empowering because it means you can identify which Destiny-Goals should not be pursued because they are impossible, and not waste time on them. But more importantly then that, something that you previously thought impossible you will now be able to perceive as possible. This in itself is a 'miracle.'

When you impose on yourself a limitation, it holds you back. When you remove the limitation, you can continue forward to pursue your destiny!

As a final footnote. People can't re-grow a lost arm, but experimental medical science has meant that a donor arm can be attached and function fully. Also. Medical science cannot resurrect the dead, but every day there are hundreds, if not thousands, of people who technically die, their hearts stops, or they stop breathing, yet they are resuscitated. It seems sometimes even the impossible is possible.

Rahul was a friendly young elephant, and an only calf. He was often visited by a flock of parakeets and they would all play in the streams of his homeland. They would share gossip about the greedy politician and his pernicious wife, they would tell jokes about the snake with the stiff neck, and they all laughed so hard when discussing the bullying tiger that was tricked into marrying a monkey. But everyday, when sunset came, the birds would fly away to enjoy their evening sky-games. Rahul was always left standing alone as he stared enviously as the parakeets disappeared on the horizon. He would wonder what it would be like to fly like them. One day he declared that he would fly! He stood at the edge of a steep hill, jumped, and flapped his legs like wings. THUMP! He fell and bashed his skull. A pride of tig-monks laughed at him. His pride hurt more than his head. Simil, the eldest of the Parakeets had been watching. Sympathetically he asked 'what's wrong my big grey friend?' Rahul said 'I wanted to be a bird. I wanted to know what it would be like to fly like you and all the other parakeets. I thought that if I did my highest jump I would be able to.' Simil's eyes softened. 'My friend, it's good to wonder about different things. But you body was never meant to fly like a bird. However not a day passes where the other parakeets say to me what a fine example of an elephant you are. Of all our friends only you can stomp your feet so hard that it makes a noise like monsoon thunder. Only you have a trunk that you can shoot water like rain. Only you have a noble roar that scares away any attackers. We know that in your company you will always protect us. That is why we call you friend.' Rahul started smiling again. Simil jumped onto his back and Rahul walked up to the tig-monks who were still tittering. Rahul took a deep intake of breath, and then roared the loudest roar he ever did make. The tig-monks all ran off frightened with their monkey tails between their stripy legs. Rahul and Simil laughed until tears came out of their eyes.

So Much to Fear –Let Courage Guide you

"For all sad words of tongue and pen, The saddest are these, 'It might have been.' "

- John Greenleaf Whittier

Every single person takes their journey through life with hope and expectancy for the future. We like to see ourselves as discerning adults who have the intelligence and wisdom to deal with any situation. But no matter how au-fait we believe we are to the ways of the world, there will come times when we don't have the answers, when we're not sure what to do and for an adult this is a very unsettling experience. Sometimes it feels like we are children who have escaped through the back gate of *our* father's house. We suddenly feel very alone, fearful, and unsure of the world and our place in it. The bottom line is that *life can be scary.*

People allow their lives to become a series of routines. You wake up, you go to work. You do a job you're bored sick of, you work your guts out, and its never appreciated. You have no prospects. You come home. You do this five days a week. At the weekend you spend 'quality time' with a partner, in a relationship you suspect died long ago. Or week in week out, you go out to the same places to socialise. You see the same people, you talk about the same things. And things never change, and you never quite feel happy. You know you want more out of life. You have Destiny-Goals!

But no one is going to suddenly turn up at you house, knock on the door, and when you answer *say 'Here's a lot of money, here's the deeds for a new home, here's a contract for a high paid and enjoyable job, here's a beautiful person who will love you.'* This doesn't happen. You have to actively pursue your own Destiny-Goals. For only you have the means to make this all happen.

It is common for people to experience doubt when faced with the opportunity to make changes that could bring them closer to their Destiny-Goals. They know what they want to do. What they should do. But faced with an actual decision. Their legs shake. They balk. Their will crumbles. Its easier to turn up to a job you hate, then to face rejection when looking for a new job. Its easier to lie to yourself and your partner about a failing relationship then it is to break up and feel heartache for the sake of the long-term happiness of the both of you. Its easier to stay in, or only ever socialise in the same way, then it is to move out of your comfort zone to interact with new and different people in diverse and wondrous places.

When making changes in life, you will wonder how things might turn out, you will question the outcome, if it will be for better or worse. *Fear* is a safety measure built into all humans. If you have a fear of heights you don't allow yourself to travel too far above ground level. In this way, your fear is a safety feature that prevents you from falling and dying. Now this fear is helpful if it means it stops you from making dangerous decisions like jumping off a high cliff. But if it means you cannot work in a penthouse office which you reach via an elevator or you are unable to experience the wonder of travelling to other countries via an aeroplane then it means your fear restricts you and the decisions you make. Likewise people experience fear when faced with making an important decision. This is *emotional fear*, the fear of being emotionally hurt. The fear of failure.

'What if I ask her out and she turns me down. I'm not sure I could handle that rejection.'

'What if I ask for a pay rise and I don't get it. I don't want him to be condescending to me'

What if I ask a question and get it wrong. I don't want the others to laugh at me.'

Emotional fear is entwined with vanity. One of the deepest wounds you can inflict on a person is one on their pride or self-image. We see ourselves as fragile creatures. But;

You are not fragile! You are a strong bold individual!

Failure wont kill you! It wont even damage you. The thing is life isn't supposed to be easy. Making important decisions is not easy. Its okay to be scared, its absolutely normal to feel scared. Its human! Of course nobody likes to 'fail.' But people want to spare themselves this anguish. They don't want to 'rock the boat.' So they don't pursue their Destiny-Goals. Others have their Destiny-Goals delivered to their feet, and they turn away from it because they lack courage!

Bernadette is a beautiful but bashful young woman who has been living with Nathanial for eighteen months. When she moved in with him she felt very positive about the relationship. Not long after he became controlling, domineering and insecure. He stopped her from socialising with her friends, and even prevented her from visiting her family. Subsequently the relationship stalled emotionally, and physically it was a complete disaster. Despite this, she put her hope into the relationship and asked him to marry her, he refused because of commitment issues. Although she cares deeply for Nathanial the love she has for him is more like that a sister has for a brother. Countless days and nights pass where she finds herself thinking back to her dreams of finding true love, and enjoying life a little bit more. One day she makes a Cosmic Order for a man to walk into her life who will love her, cherish her and actually want to marry her. She then forgets about her Cosmic Order and returns to her unfulfilling home life. Then one day Michael, a very handsome and charismatic man starts working at her place of employment. They decide to go to lunch together, they talk and they are both immediately enraptured. Their hearts beat faster. They are both smitten! At the end of the working day he goes home and phones all his friends to say "I've met the woman I want to marry!" He then dances joyously around the house. Bernadette is also totally love-struck. She knows Michael desires her physically and emotionally, she knows he wants to marry her. She feels the same! She made an Order from the Cosmos and she has been given exactly what she asked for! It's what she wants! Her chance for a happy fulfilling life filled with a deep love is right in front of her. She knows what she must do. She must go home explain to Nathanial that their relationship has grounded, and that she doesn't see a long-term future together. But she doesn't do this. She doesn't end her relationship with Nathanial because she doesn't want to hurt his feelings, she doesn't want an argument. Instead she betrays her dreams and takes the cowardly root. She spurns Michael's advances. With a heavy heart she mourns the happy life she might have had, and will go on to waste the best years of her life, indoors, with a man who doesn't actually know her, and could never truly love her.

There is a genuinely sad misconception humanity has. It is, that if you try to achieve something, whether its a task or within a relationship, and you don't 'succeed' then you are a failure. Quite simply. This is WRONG! In a world filled with infinite variables and interactions even the greatest of self-actualising and high-achieving people wont 'succeed' in every endeavour all the time otherwise they would be an infallible god. The truth is;

<u>If you do not even attempt to try the tasks and challenges you face in life you are the ultimate failure. And the person you have wronged most is yourself.</u>

If you turn away from situations where you can 'fail,' although you may feel you are sparing yourself the pain of failure, what actually happens is far worse. An inner doubt gnaws at you, unbeknownst, it eats away at your confidence. You lose respect for yourself, and belief in yourself. You live in a cocoon of a world. Neither do you make decisions nor do you want to. You shy away from life. You avoid situations for fear of being judged.

<u>When you relinquish control of your life you live like a dogs in his master's house- you will never be anything more than a subservient pet.</u>

Dogs eat when their master gives them food, they sleep when they are told to, they even play at the bequest of their master. Who are people's masters? Anyone and everyone. Husbands, wives, boyfriends, girlfriends, colleagues, boss, family, business, people in the street. When you live without courage you unknowingly behave in a way that sends out permission for others to take advantage of you. This is no way to live! There is a better way to live!

Its not to say people who do have Destiny-Goals are fearless and without doubt. Of course everyone feels fear and doubt, but you mustn't let it consume you else it hijacks the way you behave in your life. To be apprehensive about the outcome of a situation is normal. But you must not then fall prey to it. Feel fear, okay, but look at the whole picture and work through it. Don't turn away and regret what you never did and never tried.

You are strengthened when you have a clear vision of your Destiny-Goals

Be vigilant against disclosing your Destiny-Goals to those without these hopes. Although they are the sort to always be laughing and smiling – *don't be fooled.* They are shrouded in an aura of pessimism. The minute you reveal you have hopes of changing aspects of your life they will involuntarily dissuade you. Involuntary because they are not doing so out of spite or malice, rather through an inability to see beyond the status quo. They fear change. If you are a sailboat on your journey of self-discovery, then they steal the wind from your sails. It may be that you talk about your hopes or aspirations and they say "chance would be a fine thing" or "not ruddy likely." Anything that will knock your confidence.

Don't tell anyone about your Destiny-Goals if you feel uncomfortable about doing so, even if it's a loving spouse. You do not need to hear a 'rational opinion' from a friend. There is a time for being rational and that is when making rational, cool, calm and collected decisions. Destiny-Goals are not about being cool. They are about inspiration. Running, jumping, and trying to touch the sky. Hearing a dispassionate opinion may knock your confidence and deflate the imperative and the emotion you have for it. You must not let their pessimism infect your desire to achieve your destiny.

Don't share with others your Destiny-Goals unless you can be sure of their absolute and complete support.

It is when you are most vulnerable that you need courage the most.

When you step outside your comfort zone. In an environment or situation that makes your heart pound in panic. When you are fearful of being hurt, fearful of change, fearful of failing. Having courage is not a lack of fear. Having courage is when you stand up to the challenge _despite_ your fear for the purpose of achieving a greater goal, your Destiny-Goals. By fighting through the darkness of fear with your bravery you will be able to propel yourself in new directions. And the rewards will be a feeling of such overwhelming pride in yourself, it will be nothing short of emotional nectar!

Shanequa and Panjeet are two close friends both have an interview for the same very administration job. It is well paid with good perks. Shanequa thinks the interviewer will judge her on her hairstyle or be overly critical of her experience. She doesn't want to be refused the job. To save herself the emotions of rejection she doesn't bother to go to the interview. Panjeet is equally qualified. She also feels very nervous about the interview. She prepares her clothes the night before, goes to bed early but has a restless sleep. She travels by train to the interview and is slightly late. She chats to the secretary, and the other applicants. Goes into the interview. Nervously answers some tough questions. Goes homes exhausted. Next day she gets a phone call to say that she did not get the job. Understandably she is disappointed. Shanequa phones and says 'I told you, you wouldn't get it. You could have saved yourself money, time, and the rejection.' But Panjeet thinks that if the odds of getting a job are one in every 10 interviews, she sees herself as a step closer to her goal. A week later she goes to another job interview. Aware that she might not get it she still wants to do the best she can. Learning from her last interview she catches an earlier train. She arrives at the interview with time to spare. She smiles at the receptionist. She has another tough interview but this time answers the questions more confidently. When she gets home she reflects on her day. Panjeet doesn't know if she will get the job, but she does know that the interview went well. She did the best she could, and if she doesn't get it, she will have even more experience for her next interview. She goes to bed knowing that it is only a matter of time before she gets her dream job.

Using Cosmic Ordering Against Others.

"He who seeks vengeance must dig two graves, one for his enemy and one for himself."

– ancient Chinese proverb.

The Earth has a living space that is shared by billions of people. The beauty of humanity is that each person has their own opinions, aspirations and emotions. When there is disagreement between people, as often happens, it is inevitable that conflict will arise. In your life other people may upset you, make you mad, angry and physically hurt you. When this happens you feel aggrieved and a deep sense of injustice. But when 'the world' doesn't provide any helpful solutions to your conflict it is natural to ask, can you use the power of Cosmic Ordering against others? The short answer is yes. Definitely. *But do you really want to?* If you are sure you want to do so you must first decide whose life you want to disrupt and how. When striving to achieve something for yourself this is called a Destiny-Goal. But words as noble as Destiny-Goal are not appropriate when seeking to harm others. Instead these are known as Harm-Goals.

You make your demand of the Cosmos by following The Seven Stages of Cosmic Ordering, and connecting to energy of the Cosmos. That means you write your Harm-Goals in your Cosmic Journal, you visualise them, emotionalise them, you talk to the Cosmos about them, you carry reminder symbols and you have faith. This entire process means that instead of becoming *destiny conscious* you become *harm conscious*. This is how you connect to the Cosmos. But instead of channelling positive energy and emotions it is all negative. If you order someone ill-health, bad luck, unhappiness and such like you are making a regular, conscious, and voluntary decision to focus on negativity. This always has consequences.

When you do a kind, helpful or charitable deed how does it make you feel? Probably quite nice. Okay people do good for altruistic reasons but there is absolutely no harm in admitting that it makes you feel great inside! So by helping others you are actually improving your own well being. Even if its in a small way, you make your corner of the world a better place.

Our thoughts to others and how we treat others has a direct affect on how we feel.

Likewise, when your thoughts are permanently in a realm of hate. When you think about bringing and causing upset or pain to others how does it make you feel? Surprisingly, not very good. You may clench your fist, grit your teeth, swear, growl. It's *you* who gets angry. But your *harm consciousness* ends up consuming *you*.

Every time you act on this hate you stain your hands with the blood of your sins, and the blood of your victims.

It doesn't make you feel better it makes you feel worse. There comes a point where you classify yourself as being bad. And then its hard to change that opinion of yourself or redeem yourself in your own eyes.

When you use Cosmic Ordering to harm others it tarnishes your soul

Using Cosmic Ordering against others may bring you what you perceive to be 'justice' against another. But your subjective view of justice is likely to be out of synchronisation with the Cosmos. When you instigate harm against others, you are inviting negativity into your life. Be sure of this. Whether now or later, *balance* will come.

Persian fables tell of Djinn, evil spirits imprisoned in lamps for an eternity so as to keep them away from humanity. Once in a while a hapless peasant would discover the lamp, rub it and free the Djinn who would be so grateful for this temporary freedom that he would grant his rescuer three wishes. Now whilst these wishes seemed heaven sent, it was not without good reason that the Djinn had been imprisoned. The Djinn would grant every wish literally thus he would find a verbal 'loophole' that would actually make the wishes more of a curse.

Al-Chubb was a peasant who worked on the fields of his master Kharim. Kharim always showed him kindness, giving him warm soft bread and refreshing goat's milk or paying him extra dinars for good work. Despite such compassion Al-Chubb would often spend his days glaring at Kharim with pernicious eyes, hiding his spite with a mask of smiles. When he saw how Kharim never dirtied his hands in work, he despised him for it. When he looked enviously at Kharim's stately home, he would curse about it. However Al-Chubb's worst crime was always committed when Kharim's beautiful wife Amineh walked passed, he would shamelessly lust for her.

One day when Al-Chubb was turning over the field, his

spade hit something. He stopped to look and discovered a fine bejewelled golden lamp. His eyes bounced open as he realised that he could sell it for a fine sum of money. As he rubbed the mud away to get a better look at it, it started shaking in his hand, he heard a rumbling inside, a voice? 'AAAGGGHHH!' He dropped it and a black cloud shot out of the spout and formed into the most scrawny Djinn imaginable. "I am the Djinn Matchisar and I grant you three wishes." Al-Chubb couldn't believe his luck, he look at his dirty hands, then at the stately home of Kharim, then back at his hands and hastily said "I want to never have to work again. I want to be ruler of my own kingdom where I am the king and master, and I want to take Kharim's beautiful wife as my own." The Djinn gave a sly smile and said "Your wishes are my command" he then clapped his hands and Al-Chubb couldn't see for a giant cloud of black smoke.

When the smoke cleared he could see he was in a majestically decorated chamber in a very fine bed. This was obviously the palatial bedroom. His wishes had come true! He went to step out of the bed. BANG. He fell out on to the floor and cut his head. Puzzled he looked down at himself and saw he had no legs. In this state he realised he would never work the fields again. But then he remembered his second wish had obviously come true, he was king of his own kingdom so he wouldn't need to work! He crawled over to the wall and pushed opened the blinds. As he stared out he saw nothing but desert. This was his kingdom but no one lived in it. Because he had no citizens it meant he had no taxes. He was a dinar-less king! He then struggled to climb up to the summit of a chair. The door then burst open it was Amineh. "Thank the heavens" said Al-Chubb in relief, "My beautiful wife, come to me. For I am your new husband!" He was eagerly looking forward to bedtime. Amineh stared around the room and sized up her predicament. She was as wise as she was beautiful and faithful. Only ten minutes before she had been indoors about to eat lunch with Kharim when she suddenly disappeared and reappeared in this palace. Although she did not know what exactly had happened she saw the lecherous look on Al-Chubb's face. She went over to him. Slapped him so hard he fell on the floor again, and left to get the horse from the stable to ride back to her husband. As blood poured into his eyes a bewildered Al-Chubb was left staring at the ceiling of his palace that stood in a desert kingdom where nobody lived.

Cosmic Healing

Cosmic Ordering is a powerful force that can bring positive change into your life by affecting people and events around you as well as developing your perception of the world. But at times you may have more humble aspirations; to change an aspect of your existence that is much closer to home, and more central to the quality of your life – your health.

The modern era has brought so many improvements to modern life, however this is offset by its own share of *modern illness*. We have technological 'solutions' for everyday tasks that should make life effortless. We have dish-washers to clean our plates, cars that allow us to travel great distances in little time, computers that enable us to work from home. Life should be getting easier but instead more and more people are suffering from stress, and in extreme cases, depression.

There are many other modern sicknesses that people inflict upon themselves. Food and drink is the body's fuel, enjoyed sensibly it represents a delicious celebration of life. Yet there are many who consume food to an unnecessary level of excess. There is nothing wrong with overindulging occasionally. But some people eat too much, others aren't just overweight, they are morbidly obese. Their blood pressure rises, their stamina falls, they increase the risk of suffering from a number of related illnesses such as diabetes, and alarmingly they dramatically increase their risk of suffering a heart attack. They eat when they're not hungry! Why do they do it? Is it a fear that the food will run out, and they are trying to consume as much as possible before it does? This would be a compelling argument if the person was from a country were food is scarce, and where there is always a question as to where their next meal will come from. But in the west, food is not scarce .

Perversely in a society that is characterised by its abundance, considering there is no danger of there being a shortage of food in the western world, some people are going to the other extreme and voluntarily starving themselves. They choose to override their biological need for food by restricting and controlling what they allow into their bodies. In the process, they starve themselves of nutrition and protein and life-giving fuel. Their weight falls to dangerous levels, their hair thins out, their face goes sallow, the enamel flakes from their teeth. In short, their bodies slowly shut down on them…

Likewise people choose to put narcotic substances into their bodies, which have no biological benefit, for the sake of 'recreation' without acknowledging they are slowly poisoning themselves. Besides these conditions the more traditional illnesses still afflict us. The common cold, the flu, and the scourge of the human body - cancer. There are so many illnesses that affect the quality of the human life.

Any health problem will be especially harmful if our bodies are weak, and this tends to happen when we are suffering from stress. Stress is when we feel emotional or physical tension in response to particular stimuli. It is a function of the human body that allows us to better deal with dangerous situations. For example if you are confronted by a mugger carrying a knife, the stress will cause the release of the adrenaline hormone into your body. This in turn has the effect of heightening your senses, your heart will beat faster, you will hear better, see better, move faster. So if the mugger tries to stab you, your heightened awareness will help you to avoid his strike. Or if you try to punch him, you will hit him with an especially strong blow. The adrenalin gives your body an energy boost to help you come out of the situation alive, however when it does this your immune system works at a fraction of its normal effectiveness leaving your body in a weakened state. Then, when you are safely out of the situation the adrenaline stops being released, and your body needs rest as you are left feeling exhausted.

It is not just physical danger that makes us feel stress its also other factors that we experience on a day to day basis such as financial worries or concerns about a relationship. This has the effect of putting are bodies under almost continual stress, and it means our immune systems are always weakened meaning we are far more susceptible to illness. What might be normally be regarded as a minor health problem can take a far more serious toll on the body.

So what does everyone do when they get sick? They rush to their doctor for 'treatment.' So if you are overeating, the doctor can give you a drink to make your body think you are not hungry. If you suffer from nervousness, your doctor can give you a pill to 'steady your nerves,' and when people have things going on in their life that make them sad, makes them cry and leaves them feeling depressed doctors give them narcotics to chemically trick them into thinking they are happy!

THIS ISN'T HEALING. This is just using medicine to treat the symptoms and not the problems. Of course such modern medicine does have its benefits in that it can offer patients relief from their ailments, but this relief is just a short-term solution. It masks the underlying health problem without trying to deal with treating the cause.

What is the root cause of most modern illness? Most often the cause is unsettled problems of the heart. *Problems of the heart* are emotionally upsetting issues that have been suppressed by the sufferer to spare themselves anguish. They stem from negative life experiences that have been particularly traumatic. Whether it be incidents of name-calling, bullying, frightening situations, or physical violence. A vicious dog barking at a child might manifest itself in later life as a fear of animals. Or a young toddler distressed by a regularly absent parent may grow up lacking in self-confidence and develop insecurities. To one degree or another everyone has such issues. If our psyche isn't too wounded then it doesn't leave much of a lasting imprint, but when it is hurt, it affects our entire character by hampering our ability to deal with problematic situations. So does this mean that you can't eliminate body-weakening stress because it is purely a consequence of the problems you face in life? Does it mean that if you didn't have these problems you wouldn't feel stress? NO! Most people have life problems of one sort or another. What makes everyone different is our individual propensity to deal with stress. When faced with stress some people handle stress well, other people fall apart at the seams. That is why one person can keep calm under the most testing of circumstances whilst another gets heated over the most petty matters. If you spend some time in any business and observe the behaviour of the management; you will see for yourself how some always seem to be calm in disposition, whilst others seem to run around, continually stressed and often shouting unnecessarily. Therefore to improve your ability to deal with stress you have to face up to the problems of your heart. Cosmic Healing can help you do this.

Cosmic Healing is when you use the power of Cosmic Ordering to improve your health and wellbeing. Cosmic Healing does not combat nature, nor is it a 24 hour cure for defective DNA or any of the diseases it may have lying in wait for you. The power of Cosmic Healing comes from its ability to make sure you are in the sharpest mental condition, most emotionally stable, and least stressed condition you can be in. When you are in your physical and mental peak, it means you will have the strength to fight some illness that otherwise you might not have. Of course modern medicine can help tremendously, but this alone is not enough. If it was everyone who goes into hospital for a curable disease would come out cured, but this doesn't happen.

Again you are required to follow the 7 Stages of Cosmic Ordering, but much more emphasis is to made on *Stage 4 – Talk to the Cosmos*. This is because Cosmic Healing is less about the external world, and much more about you focusing on the inner state of your heart and body. When you begin Stage 4 make sure you are in a comfortable place where you wont be disturbed. Close yours eyes and *trust*. Confide in the Cosmos as if it is your closest most faithful friend sitting in the room next to you.

In modern living when talking about problems there is a tendency to use platitudes to spare any hurt to the feelings of others. Why call a person fat when its nicer to call them big-boned? This is done with noble intent but it is dangerous because it's a denial of a problem. The implicit meaning of these platitudes is that when it comes to maintaining good health, there is no right or wrong. This is a fallacy, and its stops people acknowledging a problem and so they don't deal with it. The problem then festers in the soul to become a problem of the heart.

> ***When you willingly discuss with the Cosmos the life experiences and traumas that have left an indelibly harmful mark on your psyche, no matter how difficult this might be, it immediately starts the healing process for your heart.***

So when talking to the Cosmos acknowledge any problems within your heart that trouble you, *be honest*. The very act of Cosmic Ordering will give you the strength to do so. So if you have a weight problem and you like to describe yourself as cuddly, DON'T. Admit that you are fat.

Does being fat make you evil? - Of course not.

Does it mean you don't have feelings? – definitely not.

Does being fat make you unattractive? – beauty is in the eye of the beholder, and there is always someone for everyone!

Does being fat affect your health? -Yes.

Does being fat make you more prone to diabetes, high blood pressure, joint stiffness and more -YES

Does being fat make you die quicker? -DEFINITELY.

Does being fat mean you will have less years with your loved ones then you would have if you were otherwise healthy? - YES. DEFINITELY YES.

Admitting a problem will upset you, it may make you sad. but it will be cathartic. The Cosmos responds to truth; when you are in situations that might detrimentally affect your well-being, it will give you guidance. More importantly it will work through you and give you the strength to act on that guidance. In the instance where you suffer from an excessive weight problem there is so much information readily available to you from the media that you most likely know what is helpful to you and what is harmful. When you discuss your problems you lessen them and the Cosmos will give you the vigour to act. Instead of having a second piece of cake you will stop and be content with what you had. Instead of thinking about joining a gym, you will pack a gym bag and go there with your bank account details. Hence the Cosmos will aid you to take small steps of action that are insignificant by themselves, but cumulatively work in your favour. When you face these issues you are removing the emotional burdens that impinge on your life, and you will discover this is an exhilarating feeling.

After *talking to the Cosmos* the healing process is magnified by a simple but powerful *Cosmic Meditation* technique that will promote good health by fortifying your healthy cells.

An Introductory Cosmic Meditation.

Close your eyes, if they're not already closed. Slowly take seven deep breaths, this will relax your body and slow down your mind. Then, continue to breath deeply. Imagine the inside of your body, imagine the energy inside as being a fine white mist circulating around it. This energy is the life-giving fuel that powers your body. See it flow from your fingertips up your arm to your neck, up to your head, down your chest, through your beating heart, down to your legs down, to your toes and then around again. Feel the warm feeling of the energy, full of nourishing nutrients and vitamins to feed your body. Then picture your bad health condition as a small cloud of black mist.

See how this mist is the cause of your problem. This black mist is a poison you won't bare any longer. It is time to remove it from your body. Your body is filled with white energy circulating around it. You can control it to help yourself. Use the energy to surround the black mist, squashing it, squeezing it, and pushing up to your skin, and out of your body. See the black mist dissipate into the air. Your body is now bursting with positive energy.

Through the entire process the body learns to heal itself starting from the mind moving down to the body, giving your immune system a massive power-up.

Use Cosmic Healing to help you face the problems in your heart to make you emotionally happier. When your heart is content your body will strengthen and your health will improve. This is as good a reason as any to celebrate!

A Time for Reflection

"Life isn't a matter of milestones but of moments"
– Rose Fitzgerald Kennedy

When you have definite Destiny-Goals you are empowering yourself to manoeuvre your life in the direction you want, so that you attain what you have always dreamed of. But Destiny-Goals do not materialise overnight. It would be lovely if you made a Cosmic Order, and after a day or two a Destiny-Goal of yours was fulfilled! Now this does happen. Especially for the smaller more modest Orders. But most Destiny-Goals take a little more time. If, for example, you have hopes of finding a marriage partner, or finding a new job, or saving ten million, you might not see resolutions for months or years.

The danger is that you may focus purely on whether you have achieved a Destiny-Goal or not. Remaining *Destiny-Goal conscious* is good. But if you get so caught up pursuing them that you neglect the joys of everyday living this can have a detrimental effect on the way you feel.

When you use the power of Cosmic Ordering you do so optimistically but this often contrast greatly with the mundane and practical realities of your everyday life. You may well be *Destiny-Goal conscious* looking forward to a financially strong future but then the post is delivered and you see you have a pile of outstanding bills to pay. Or perhaps you want an appealing social life which you have taken steps to improve. You are looking forward to attending a party with a friend but they cancel at the last minute. It can be extremely frustrating when you compare your surroundings with the life you hope to live. When you do this you just feel tense and impatient. One of the strengths of the human condition is that when we are going through difficult or upsetting times, we can get through it by letting our thoughts visit a future time where things are better. But having a better, happier, more rewarding life is not a specific day in the future where magically, bish-bash-bosh, suddenly you have money, and true love, and a happy ending. If you continually think like this you neglect the day-to-day decisions of your life that will get you there.

There is great adage *'Success is not a journey, it's a destination.'* This is absolutely spot on. Progress is made every day in small steps. If you go to the beach and swim out to sea in a straight line. If after 500 metres, you stop and look back you will see that, without realising it, you have actually deviated sideways significantly from your starting point. You have made incremental shifts in your direction which were not noticeable at the time. This is exactly how it is with your Destiny-Goals. Don't be impatient. Acknowledge your minor successes. So every time that you can see that you are a step closer to your goal give yourself a pat on the back. Congratulate yourself! When you know you are on the right path to achieving your Destiny-Goals you will attract more positive energy and feel compelled to progress even further.

When you do achieve a Destiny-Goal. Its so rewarding. Exalt in it, allow the feelings of pride to intoxicate you!

Look forward to the future but don't live in it. Your life is NOW! THIS day! TODAY. Enjoy it!

Whispers in the Wind

Using Cosmic Ordering to realise your Destiny-Goals can make a fantastic difference to your life. Use it effectively and you will develop a healthy obsession with results. But once in a while it's worth taking a 'time-out' to step back and observe and wonder about the source of the Cosmic powers. Rather then specifically planning to this, you will learn that this experience happens to you unexpectedly, completely out of the blue.

Whispering in the Wind is similar to the Sixth Stage of Cosmic Ordering whereby you *Send your Order* out to the Cosmos. But rather than actually trying to communicate a message, what you are actually doing is connecting to the energy of the Cosmos, so that you *feel* the energy of the Cosmos. *Whispering in the Wind* is never planned for. It happens suddenly, without invitation.

When you are alone and feeling contemplative. Take a walk outdoors, anywhere where there is evidence of nature and life. Near greenery, a park, near a lake. Take a slow-paced walk, look at the world with fresh eyes, and notice the detail in nature that you ordinarily take for granted. Feel the warm sun stroke your face, observe the beautiful form of birds. Marvel at the beauty and wonder of *Mother Nature*. Take a moment to look around. Once in a blue moon there is an propitious shift in the celestial movements that can actually be felt here on Earth. How do you know, by calculating charts and crunching numbers? Yes, but that can be far too niggling. You can usually recognise an auspicious time when there is a sudden shift in weather. Most often during a sunny and bright day, birds tweeting. Suddenly, within the space of five minutes the clouds darken, the birds either take flight or take cover, and there is an eerie silence in the air. Silence except for the sound of a growing wind rustling through every single leaf of every single tree. You then experience a feeling of tense expectation which just seems to hang before a violent rainstorm hits.

Listen carefully. Listen to the sound of the wind in the trees. If you listen hard enough you will hear the wind carrying the secret whispers of billions of other hearts all calling out at once. Some shouting, some laughing, some crying. Hopes longed for, promises made, love yearned for, dreams shattered. Don't ask, don't speak, don't send, *just listen* to the secrets, *just feel*. Of course you wont be able to understand what is being said. But the emotions are universal, and their voices are unmistakable. Try to understand if you must, but when your vanity is humbled *stop*, and be content to know that you have reached out and *stroked* the underbelly of the Cosmos.

If you listen Whispers in the Wind also come when the sun is at its most evocative. We all know the sun is most powerful during the day. Bright. Life-giving. Anonymous. Then there are sunsets. Have you ever wondered why some people, maybe yourself, seem to be enraptured by sunsets? What is it about them that seems to send the human soul into a delirious flight of emotions? Why is it that when a perfectly sane man, strolling down the beach with a woman, sees the sun set, and all of a sudden he's professing to hold her hand until the end of time uttering 'I am yours and you are mine?' What makes an otherwise intelligent career woman, well educated, intellectual, see a sunset and suddenly she dreams of giving up work for a fairytale happy ever after with Prince

Charming. Or even more enigmatic than that is the behaviour of a pre-teen boy. Twelve years old, ordinarily preoccupied with dreams of owning the newest PlayStation games console, he suddenly catch a glimpse of a ruby sunset and his heart alternately lifts high with hopes then falls with a deep ache. His life experiences have been limited, yet his heart aches with a wisened yearning and melancholy and he has no comprehension as to why.

Certain meteorological conditions, such a different hue in the sky, switch off our propensity to run on 'autopilot.' We stop being so focused on our internal world and begin to observe the surroundings of the outside world.

The skies elicit from us an emotional response. The different hues tap into something primeval about us. A truth buried deep within the memories of our souls. A feeling or a knowledge of time when there were no distractions. Just humans. Under a naked sky. When you listen to the Whispers in the Wind you start noticing the majesty of nature's beauty, of the skies, the Cosmos, and the entwined history you share with every single organism that has ever lived. *When you do this you become the Cosmos.*

Organised Religion & Cosmic Ordering

No matter what part of the world you are from you are likely to have been raised with an awareness of one of the mainstream religions. They are also known as organised religions because they have a rich amount of historical dogma as well as firmly established hierarchical systems for both their religious leaders and their places of worship, be it priest, brahmin, mullah or monk. These organised religions have varying but very specific views on their respective faiths; the details which serve to answer how the world was made, by whom, who the Supreme Being is, how morality works, if there is an afterlife and how that works, what is good and what is evil.

Cosmic Ordering encompasses a great many philosophical and scientific schemas. It looks at the planets in our Solar System, the sun signs of the zodiac and how their movements correlate with geographical and human behaviours on Earth. It comprises the Theory of Everything, and synchronicity and these all illuminate an understanding of the Cosmos that is all powerful and supreme.

If you have a strong religious faith yet desire to harness the power of Cosmic Ordering, it can be difficult to reconcile the two belief systems. This doesn't need to be the case. *The Ultimate Guide to Cosmic Ordering* does not set out to challenge or contradict any faith, rather Cosmic Ordering is an understanding of the infinite and unexplainable power within the universe and how it can be utilised for self-empowerment.

Astrology in particular raises questions for Christians, and some other faiths, who have beliefs based on mankind's free will to make their own decisions and affect their own lives. God and astrology are sometimes regarded as being mutually exclusive. How can their be a God, creator of the Cosmos, and a God creator of the zodiac and sun signs that give insights on people's lives. How can God, astrology, and Cosmic Ordering co-exist? *How can they not?!*

There was once a time when people believed that Science and God could not co-exist. The principle was that if there are scientific rules to explain physical phenomena then this contradicts the idea of a God whose 'power' makes things happen. Thus the existence of one disproves the existence of the other. Nowadays this opinion has mostly been abandoned for being too simplistic. There are few believers in God who would deny the laws of science such as gravity, genetic inheritance, or of photosynthesis. Also there are many scientist who do have a faith in God. The two theories can co-exist because its possible for God to have created a world. A world which there are rules, physics, scientific principles, laws and *himself!*

If science is compatible with God, then surely its possible for *how* the planets and stars operate to be entwined with an overall design also created by God? Planets are just another element of the unexplained phenomena but linked with everything else *he* created. The movements of the planets can be interpreted as being the mechanical workings of the heavens, another Science which we are still in the process of understanding.

If God created the Earth, and us, its only logical that he created the Sun and the rest of our universe as they are all part of a unified solar system. They are all part of the

Cosmos. Thus the universe will undoubtedly bare the signature of the creator. Yet scientists continually demand answers as to how the planets interact with humans. There is nothing wrong with this. To desire greater knowledge on these subjects is fantastic. Its what humans strive to do. Learn and understand. But mankind is not all knowing. All around the world scientific discoveries, both small and big are made every week, and will continue to be made for many, many more years to come. Scientist are continually learning more about how the world 'works.' As a species we don't have all the answers now. So if mankind hasn't even discovered a single percent of the knowledge of Earth, its people, and the laws of physics, then it will be even more difficult to comprehend the facts about planets and stars which are hundreds, thousands, and millions of miles away. So really it's quite arrogant for us to say that we should automatically understand the science of God in the heavens when we don't even understand all the sciences of a God on Earth.

Cosmic Ordering is not intended to challenge the histories and philosophies of the world's belief systems. Rather it compliments them as it doesn't give specific answers on who created the universe and why. This can be exasperating as our curious minds like answers! However religion and Cosmic Ordering alike share the knowledge that there is something more, something greater, an energy within the universe that is present throughout every second of our lives.

A Time for Balance

'Let the stars enlighten you, not enslave you'

-Andronicos Andronicou

The power of the Cosmos is boundless, it encompasses everything in our universe, the Sun, the Moon, the stars and all other matter. Studying the mechanisms of the heavens is a valid, relevant, and enlightening process. Scientists analyse the stars to tell us about our planet, whilst astrologers read them to tell us about our lives. As humans there are so many questions that we want answered. Not just about the Cosmos but also about our own little microcosm of life.

It's normally when we are on the cusp of making important decisions that we seek out the 'harmless' advice from astrologers and spiritual teachers, and other gurus.

Am I compatible with a new partner? Should I take this job? When is an auspicious time to marry? And there are so many mystics and stargazers who are happy to share their wisdom, and if they do so and you learn a little bit more about the sort of person that you are that's great. And if you use that knowledge to improve your life in some ways, wonderful! It means you can see how you fit into the cosmic equation and fully understand your place within it. *My star sign is Cancer? Oh that explains why I'm passionate and inspired. That must be why women flock to hear my songs! My boss said I'm too excitable at work? Maybe I should tone it down there a little bit.*

But it's when people are most emotionally vulnerable that they are most susceptible to being led by spiritual advisors and the positions of the stars. When people attach an undue significance to these life readings they become a slave to them. Do you buy the newspapers every day to read your star sign? That's fine. Do you panic if you don't read it? Do you occasionally visit a spiritual advisor? Or you regularly visit a spiritual advisor so that they can tell you what are the 'right' decisions you should make? People are far too ready to believe that their entire life has been mapped out for them. When bad things happen they say *'there was a bullet with his name on it.'* But you are not a pawn of the classical gods. When you willingly surrender the decision making process you are willingly surrendering control of your life and thus control of the direction of your life. This can be comforting for some because it means that when things go wrong they don't have to blame themselves. By doing this they are denying themselves the process of self-analysis which can lead to them changing their life for the better.

If you are walking down the road and you see an old lady. You may choose to help her cross a busy road. Alternatively you may choose to mug her by pulling out a metal bar from your jacket and smashing her violently in the face with it. Make no mistake. If you do choose the latter, its not because of the stars influence on you its because *you* chose to do so. Take responsibility for your actions.

Look and listen to the Cosmos and the secrets that it whispers to you and all mankind. Look back to see where you have come from, understand who you are, and what you want from life. Your destiny is not a pre-set pattern of events of which you are merely a passenger. The person who has the most control over your life is *you*. When you have a clear defined purpose, a mind focused on Destiny-Goals you will have the means to use Cosmic Ordering to transmute the passion of your dreams into reality. Then you really will have the power in your own hands to *change* your destiny and take it in whatever direction that you want.

Looking up to a Sunset in the Heavens.

"Standing on the Shoulders of Giants"
- Sir Isaac Newton

Once upon a time we were a species hiding in dark caves fearing everyone and everything. Food that could poison us. The sabre tooth tigers that could rip us apart. The darkness of the night sky that could consume us. Then came the discovery of fire. This miraculous innovation was the advent of cooked food, illuminated nights, and the means to scare away fierce mammals. Since then mankind has never looked back. Discovering new technologies and changing and improving lives. Each generation learning from the last, each generation building knowledge and understanding to be shared with the next who will in turn build on that. Despite this, the greatest questions are no nearer being answered then they were a thousand years ago. *Is there a God? Is there an afterlife? Is there intelligent life elsewhere in the universe? Why are we here?*

What scientists have proved is the universe is expanding. Its travelling further away from some place, and travelling closer to 'some place'

Something is definitely happening, but in a time frame that is far grander than our short human lives could ever hope to comprehend. We can't ever hope to know the direction or the purpose. As the planet travels through space and time, mankind is also on a journey of knowledge to an *ultimate enlightenment.* Whether we like it or not something is happening that we wont ever know the answer to. At least not in this life. But rather then be overawed by all this we must recognise *We* each are a small, but astoundingly important cog in an infinite Cosmic clock. We each have a place and a role.

There is so much about the world that is to be feared, there is so much to be saddened about. So much hatred. It is important that you eternally hold in your conscious mind and heart that its not all like this. From a time where people were concerned just about their own survival and well being there is the slow, but growing consciousness where mankind is genuinely beginning to have concerns, and ethics about the planet and his fellow people. Caring, not just for him or herself but for the health of people in different nations, across different oceans. Caring about the vigour of nature and the planet, about the extinction of rare species.

Of course there is still hatred and war. But don't let it stop you from seeing that there is so much love. Albeit slowly, mankind is gradually maturing, improving. How can you be sure of this? Well it all starts with *you.* You have a role to play. Cosmic Ordering provides you with a fantastic opportunity to pursue all your hopes and dreams, to make them a reality. So you want to pursue wealth, health, happiness and love? Great! Go out there, chase and pursue your destiny. Don't feel bad or guilty about improving your life. But when you experience the success of Cosmic Ordering acknowledge it. Appreciate it. Give thanks for it. When you bring positivity into your life know that you are in a wonderfully privileged position.

When you are on this journey to improving your life take time to look around at others. No matter how difficult your life may be, consider the difficulties faced by those less fortunate then yourself. Feel the aches that bruise their souls. Speculate on how you may be able to help others then act! There is an inherent good in every single one of us. Give something back to help others, and when their situation improves they can give something to others also. As time passes, Earth and everyone on it moves closer to our *ultimate enlightenment*. On that day *all* men, women, and children of the world will stand united, holding hands staring in the sky at the final crimson red sunset. By then mankind will have progressed into a wiser, more caring loving species, and what is most important is that *you* make a valuable contribution.

There is so much to do in life. But take the time to look up to the heavens, let your eyes be the tongue of your soul. Feast on the beauty of the world you live in, the universe, the Cosmos. Allow yourself to bask in the glory of love. May you fulfil your destiny and reach your *ultimate potential*. Until such times, may you have the very best of health, prosperity and happiness. ***Peace***.

Appendix: Words of Wisdom

"There is no chance, no destiny, no fate, that can circumvent or hinder or control the firm resolve of a determined soul."
-*Ella Wilcox*

The journey of a thousand miles begins with a step..
- *Lao Tzu*

Be the change you want to see in the world.
- *Mahatma Gandhi*

Every person is enthusiastic at times. One person has enthusiasm for 30 minutes; another person has it for 30 days, but it is the person who has it for 30 years who makes a success of life.

- *Edward Butler George*

Courage is resistance to fear, mastery of fear--
not absence of fear.

-*Source unknown*

Until you make the unconscious conscious, it
will direct your life and you will call it fate.

- *Carl Jung*

Do the thing you are afraid to do and the death
of fear is certain.

-*Ralph Waldo Emerson*

Before you can inspire with emotion, you must
be swamped with it yourself. Before you can
move their tears, your own must flow. To
convince them, you must yourself believe.

-*Winston Churchill*

People are just about as happy as they make up their minds to be.
-*Abraham Lincoln*

There are three kinds of people: those who make things happen, those who watch things happen, and those who wonder what happened.

-*Nicholas Butler Murray*

It is the mind that maketh good or ill, that maketh wretch or happy, rich or poor.

- *Edmund Spenser*

You see things; and you say "why?" But I dream things that never were and say "Why not?"

- *George Bernard Shaw*

It is a funny thing about life; if you refuse to accept anything but the best you very often get it.

- *W. Somerset Maugham*

Nothing can stop the man with right mental attitude from achieving his goal; nothing on earth can help the man with the wrong mental attitude.

- *Thomas Jefferson*

Determine that the thing can and shall be done, and then we shall find the way.

- *Abraham Lincoln*

A stumbling block to the pessimist is a stepping-stone to the optimist.

-*Eleanor Roosevelt*

We cannot choose our external circumstances, but we can always choose how we respond to them.

-*Epictetus*

Man often becomes what he believes himself to be. If I keep on saying to myself that I cannot do a certain thing, it is possible that I may end by really becoming incapable of doing it. On the contrary, if I shall have the belief that I can do it, I shall surely acquire the capacity to do it, even if I may not have it at the beginning.

- *Mahatma Gandhi*

Imaginary obstacles are insurmountable. Real ones aren't.

-*Source unknown*

The greatest revolution of our generation is the discovery that human beings, by changing the inner attitudes of their minds, can change the outer aspects of their lives.

- *William James*

There is nothing either good or bad, but thinking makes it so.

-*William Shakespeare*

What the caterpillar calls the end, the rest of the world calls a butterfly.

-Lao Tzu

Success is going from failure to failure without loss of enthusiasm.

- Winston Churchill

When the only tool you have is a hammer, all problems begin to resemble nails.

-Abraham Maslow

Obstacles are those frightful things you see when you take your eyes off your goal.

- Henry Ford

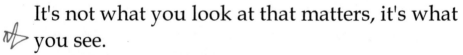It's not what you look at that matters, it's what you see.

-Henry David Thoreau

All our dreams can come true, if we have the courage to pursue them.

-*Walt Disney*

Men do not attract that which they want, but that which they are.

- *James Allen*

If one advances confidently in the direction of his dreams, and endeavours to live the life which he has imagined, he will meet with a success unexpected in common hours.

-*Henry David Thoreau*

Nothing great was ever achieved without enthusiasm.

-*Ralph Waldo Emerson*

Continuous effort - not strength or intelligence - is the key to unlocking our potential.

- *Winston Churchill*

Don't be afraid to give your best to what seemingly are small jobs. Every time you conquer one it makes you that much stronger. If you do the little jobs well, the big ones will tend to take care of themselves.

- *Andrew Carnegie*

 Our greatest glory is not in never failing, but in rising up every time we fail.

-*Ralph Waldo Emerson*

 The greatest danger for most of us is not that our aim is too high and we miss it, but that our aim is too low and we reach it.

-*Source unknown*

You cannot do a kindness too soon, for you never know how soon it will become too late.

-*Ralph Waldo Emerson*

Success doesn't mean the absence of failures; it means the attainment of ultimate objectives. It means winning the war, not every battle.

- *Edwin C. Bliss*

Dreams do come true; without that possibility, nature would not incite us to have them.

- *John Updike*

Pay no attention to what a critic says. A statue has never been erected in honour of a critic.

- *Jean Sibelius*

First, have a definite, clear practical ideal; a goal, an objective. Second, have the necessary means to achieve your ends; wisdom, money, materials, and methods. Third, adjust all your means to that end.

-*Aristotle*

The only way to have a friend is to be one.
-*Ralph Waldo Emerson*

There is only one time that is important—
NOW!! It is the most important time because it
is the only time that we have any power.
- *Leo Tolstoy*

The definition of insanity is doing the same
thing over and over again and expecting a
different result.
-*Albert Einstein*

Character may be manifested in the great
moments, but it is made in the small ones.
- *Winston Churchill*

You don't have to be great to start, but you have
to start to be great.
-*Joe Sabah*

Don't be afraid to take a big step. You can't cross a chasm in two small jumps.

- *David Lloyd George*

We are what we repeatedly do. Excellence then, is not an act, but a habit.

- *Aristotle*

The mind is its own place, and in itself, can make heaven of hell, and a hell of Heaven.

- *John Milton*

Do not follow where the path may lead. Go instead where there is no path and leave a trail.

- *Ralph Waldo Emerson*

We make a living by what we get, but we make a life by what we give.

-*Winston Churchill*

We do not act rightly because we have virtue or excellence, but we rather have those because we have acted rightly.

- *Aristotle*

As human beings, our greatness lies not so much in being able to remake the world... as in being able to remake ourselves.

- *Mahatma Gandhi*

All men seek one goal, success or happiness
   - *Aristotle*

I believe that you control your destiny, that you can be what you want to be. You can also stop and say, No, I won't do it, I won't behave his way anymore. I'm lonely and I need people around me, maybe I have to change my methods of behaving and then you do it.
-Leo F. Buscaglia

No man is great enough or wise enough for any of us to surrender our destiny to. The only way in which anyone can lead us is to restore to us the belief in our own guidance.
-*Henry Miller*

The best years of your life are the ones in which you decide your problems are your own. You do not blame them on your mother, the ecology, or the president. You realize that you control your own destiny.
-*Albert Ellis*

Courage is the discovery that you may not win, and trying when you know you can lose.
-*Tom Krause*

It is one of the most beautiful compensations of life, that no man can sincerely try to help another without helping himself.
-*Ralph Waldo Emerson*

The greatest barrier to success is the fear of failure.
-*Sven Goran Eriksson quotes*

It is a mistake to look too far ahead. Only one link of the chain of destiny can be handled at a time.
-*Winston Churchill*

He cannot complain of a hard sentence, who is made master of his own fate.
-*Johann Friedrich Von Schiller*

He that waits upon fortune is never sure of a dinner.
- *Benjamin Franklin*

Where your talents and the needs of the world cross lies your calling.
-*Aristotle*

Thoughts lead on to purposes; purposes go forth in action; actions form habits; habits decide character; and character fixes our destiny.
--*Tyron Edwards*

Upon the conduct of each depends the fate of all.
-*Alexander the Great*

Watch your words; they become actions. Watch your actions; they become habits. Watch your habits; they become character. Watch your character; it becomes your destiny.
- *Frank Outlaw*

We are all here for a spell. Get all the good laughs you can
-*Will Rogers*

Your aspirations are your possibilities.
--*Samuel Johnson*

You are today where your thoughts have brought you; you will be tomorrow where your thoughts take you.
-*James Allen*

Your living is determined not so much by what life brings to you as by the attitude you bring to life; not so much by what happens to you as by the way your mind looks at what happens.
-*John Homer Miller*

Your profession is what you were put on earth to do. With such passion and such intensity that it becomes spiritual in calling.
- *Vincent Van Gogh*

A man, when he wishes, is the master of his fate.
- *Jose Ferrer*

Character is destiny.
-*Heraclites*

Ask not what tomorrow may bring, but count a blessing every day that fate allows you.
-Horace

Because your own strength is unequal to the task, do not assume that it is beyond the powers of man; but if anything is within the powers and province of man, believe that it is within your own compass also.
-Marcus Aurelius Antoninus

Chance happens to all, but to turn chance to account is the gift of few.
-Edward Bulwer-Lytton

Control your destiny or somebody else will.
- Jack Welch

Destiny grants us our wishes, but in its own way, in order to give us something beyond our wishes.
- Goethe

We are made wise not by the recollection of our past, but by the responsibility for our future.
- *George Bernard Shaw*

We are not creatures of circumstance; we are creators of circumstance.
- *Benjamin Disraeli*

We carry with us the wonders we seek without us.
- *Thomas Browne*

We make our fortunes and we call them fate.
- *Benjamin Disraeli*

What lies behind us and what lies before us are small matters compared to what lies within us.
-*Ralph Waldo Emerson*

Man's character is his fate.
-*Heraclites*

It is not in the stars to hold our destiny but in ourselves.
- *William Shakespeare*

Success doesn't "happen". It is organized, preempted, captured, by consecrated common sense.
- *F. E. Willard*

Success is not to be pursued; it is to be attracted by the person you become.
- *Jim Rohn*

The Creator has not given you a longing to do what you have no ability to do.
-*Orison Swett Marden*

The mind of man is capable of anything because everything is in it, all the past as well as the future.
- *Joseph Conrad*

The past is like a river flowing out of sight; the future is an ocean filled with opportunity and delight.
-*Anna Hoxie*

The purpose of life, after all, is to live it, to taste experience to the utmost, to reach out eagerly and without fear for newer and richer experiences.
- *Eleanor Roosevelt*

The tallest trees are most in the power of the winds, and ambitious men of the blasts of fortune.
- *William Penn*

Every individual has a place to fill in the world, and is important, in some respect, whether he chooses to be so or not.
- *Nathaniel Hawthorne*

Fate leads the willing, and drags along the reluctant.
- *Seneca*

Find something you love to do and you'll never have to work a day in your life.
- *Harvey Mackay*

There is no such thing as chance; and what seem to us merest accident springs from the deepest source of destiny.
- *Johann Friedrich Von Schiller*

Things never go so well that one should have no fear, and never so ill that one should have no hope.
- *Turkish proverb*

Those who trust to chance must abide by the results of chance.
- *Calvin Coolidge*

The reason man may become the master of his own destiny is because he has the power to influence his own subconscious mind.
-*Napoleon Hill*

Hitch your wagon to a star.
- *Ralph Waldo Emerson*

Our destiny exercises its influence over us even when, as yet, we have not learned its nature: it is our future that lays down the law of our today.
-*Friedrich Nietzsche*

We write our own destiny . . . we become what we do.
-*Chiang Kai-shek*

For exciting Cosmic Ordering news visit...

www.CosmicOrderingOnline.com

Printed in the United Kingdom
by Lightning Source UK Ltd.
115172UKS00001B/370